This book would not be possible without the support of my son Stephen Bolden who encouraged me to challenge myself.

"If people like you, they'll listen to you but if they trust you, they'll do business with you."

--Zig Ziglar, Author, Salesman,
and Motivational Speaker

"There are two types of people who will tell you that you

cannot make a difference in this world: those who are afraid

to try and those who are afraid you will succeed."

-- Ray

Goforth

Introduction

Owning your own business is one of the greatest accomplishments an individual can experience but when you do not understand the fundamentals it can also be one of the most challenging things you can encounter. This book was written to provide some guidance as you navigate the early business landscape. It focuses on some important steps that should be taken to ensure that your business has a successful outcome. It also provides resources to help you gain access to useful tools in starting and growing your business.

As you take on this adventure please remember to continue educating yourself. Education is vital to remain relevant in your business. Take advantage of books like this, seminars, and don't be afraid of free workshops. Just because the event is free does not mean it is not valuable. Always remember you are paying with your time. The connections you can make at these events may also be priceless.

Make a Plan for Success

Have you heard the old adage if you fail to plan you have planned to fail? This is very true when you are starting a business. You need to have a business plan in place. This provides a guide as well as a realistic breakdown of the cost associated with the business. This should be prepared by you or with plenty of input from you. To receive the full benefit from a business plan you need to understand what is in it and how the information will help your business.

Some elements that should be included in your business plan are an executive summary describing the business with its location, products and services, resume of owners, the role of each owner along with their percentage of ownership. A market analysis and cost break down should also be included. Finally, a 1 year to 5 year financial projection should be included. The length depends on how far you want to plan out. Keep in mind that a business plan should be adaptable with the flexibility to change as you notice different trends in the business.

A business plan should grow with the business. It is not simply a plan for starting, but as the business grows, it should be adjusted. It should also be reviewed regularly to ensure that you are on track with your focus for the business. As the business progresses, you want to adapt an exit strategy to ensure a successful transfer or sale of the business. This is especially necessary when there are multiple owners. It allows you to consider what may happen in the event that one partner wants to exit the business or should pass. Of course, once these decisions have been decided you should obtain a legal document to protect the business.

Types of Business Plans

Informal Plan/Lean Startup Plan- A brief description of the business with its goals. This is typically one page and sometimes handwritten. Often used by the business owner as their personal guide.

Formal Business Plan/Traditional Business Plan- A detailed plan of the business consisting of an executive summary, management resumes, description of business, market analysis, services of product list, marketing and sales strategy, and financial projections.

Internal Business Plan- A plan which focuses on a particular audience within the business providing goals for that area of the business.

Strategic Business Plan- A high-level view of a company's goals and how it will achieve them. This provides a layout of the foundational plan for the entire company.

Feasibility Business Plan- Focuses on two primary questions about a business venture: who will purchase the service or product a company wants to sell and if the venture can turn a profit. Feasibility business plans include, but are not limited to, sections describing the need for the product or service, target demographics and required capital. A feasibility plan ends with recommendations for going forward.

Growth Plan- A detailed plan describing the business growth goals. It provides expansion details and financial breakdown if investors are brought into the business.

Count the Cost

Have you ever started a project and realized that you did not have enough money to cover the cost? This has happened to some business owners who did not do their research before moving forward to start a business. It is essential before you spend *any money* that you understand all of the costs associated with starting your business. You can utilize free resources like the library, local small business development centers, SCORE, women business centers, SBA and Urban League. These organizations may offer free training, mentors, market data analysis, and other resources that will help you to decide if you are ready to be a business owner.

Some cost that you will need to be aware of are related to licensing, permits, insurance, rent, equipment purchase, supplies, marketing, utilities, website design and maintenance just to name a few. These costs will be different for each business as some may operate from home while others may have rent or mortgage expenses. Whatever the case you want to make sure that you have enough to cover the cost.

To cover these costs some have used savings, crowd funding, pitch contests, insurance benefits, micro-loans, investors, and borrowed from friends and family. A combination of these methods may be needed to obtain your financial goal. Regardless of how you achieve the funds you need to make sure that you leave a little cushion to cover the unexpected.

As you contemplate the cost for your business you should utilize a projected income statement template to record your outcome.

Business Name:
Income Statement
For the Period Ended December 31, 20__

Revenues:
Net Sales	$_____
Interest Income	$_____
Total Revenues	$_____

Costs and Expenses:
Cost of Goods Sold	$_____
Salaries	$_____
Office or Store Supplies	$_____
Utilities(Power, Phone, Water)	$_____
Insurance cost	$_____
Rent	$_____
Credit Card Debt	$_____
Loans	$_____
Transportation/Travel	$_____
Adverstising/Marketing	$_____
Misc.	$_____
Total Cost and Expenses	$_____
Net Income/(Net Loss)	$_____

License the Business

The business license is an authorization issued by government agencies which allows a business or individual to operate within a specific area governed by the issuing agency. This registered document is reviewed by banks when obtaining a bank account, by lenders when obtaining financing, and by agencies when applying for permits and specific industry licenses. It is important that you monitor the expiration dates for these to ensure that you are always operating in compliance if the business is ever inspected for any reason.

The business license should include the names of all owners in the business. It will be assumed that all individuals listed on the business license are equal owners in the business thus sharing equal responsibility for the business. To prove otherwise business owners will need to have an operating agreement if they are registered as an LLC. If they are registered as a non-profit or corporation they will need bylaws stating the percentage and responsibility of each owner. It is highly recommended that you have these documents in place regardless of the percentage in ownership.

Does it matter who is listed on your business license? Yes, in most cases, everyone who owns at least 20% of the business would be required to be on a business loan. If the credit of one of the members is unsatisfactory this can override the satisfactory member and cause a decline for the loan.

Often times individuals are listed on a business license to handle the registration paper work but do not have any true function in the business. It is not necessary for them to be listed on license to register the business on behalf of the owner. Having that additional name on the license will require that you have additional documents to prove ownership should funding be required.

Document your Income

If it can't be proven on paper it did not happen. This is the viewpoint of creditors. You need to have some verifiable tracking method to validate your income. This is used to ensure your ability to afford a loan. Some methods used are bank statements, check stubs, income tax statements, 1099, W2, and SSI Income letter to name a few.

Tracking your income and expenses is not only a budgeting practice, this is useful to ensure that the business is progressing efficiently. You should have a system in place such as quick books or even an excel spreadsheet to record all income coming in or going out. You may employ a bookkeeper to record these transactions using your bank statements, however it is important that you have an understanding of what is going on with your own financials. The bookkeeper is to be used as a checks and balances option not as the only source to manage your money.

It is important that you account for all of your income on your taxes because creditors review these for trends. They want to see an increase each year in the business. You usually are allowed the largest write off the first year of the business but that should decrease as the years go by.

Similarly to creating a business plan and counting the cost, you want to plan for your loan request. You should inform your accountant of your intent so that he or she can advise you in your tax preparation.

Your Business and Credit

It has often been said that you are your business. This is true when it comes to establishing credit for a business. The business does not have any credit in the early stages so your personal credit is used to determine your credit worthiness. This often remains the case as your business begins to develop. A creditor will often review your personal credit before extending you a loan.

In reviewing your credit a creditor is going to look at several factors such as:

Are you paying your current obligations on time? Late payments or slow pays are considered a red flag and may be an indicator of poor money management.

Do you have outstanding collections or write offs?   A creditor wants to know how you treated your creditors in the past. They assume you are going to treat them the same way. It is highly recommended that if you have the ability to settle past debts or pay them completely off that you do so. Keep all records of these types of payments so that if they ever try to bring up the charge again you have documentation of your payment.

Are you maxed out? If you have utilized the total amount available to you and have no room to access anymore this is another indicator that you may be in trouble financially. This raises the question if you are not able to pay this balance down how will you be able to handle new debt.

Are you shopping for credit? Numerous inquiries on a credit report may trigger questions as to the reason for the numerous credit pulls. A creditor may wonder if you were approved for a new trade line which can affect your ability to pay additional debt.

Do you have recent credit? When you have acquired recent debt especially large ones a creditor may want to see that you are able to pay that successfully for 6 months to 1 year before they will be willing to extend to you additional debt.

What type of credit is being reported? What are your trade lines? Are there various types such as a mortgage, revolving credit, term loan, open lines of credit? The more diverse the more favorable it is viewed. For instance, if a person's credit consists of only student loan debt that has been in deferment or forbearance, a lender may be hesitant because there is no activity to review. This is not to encourage you to obtain debt but to enlighten you as to what creditors are looking at.

What is your high credit? How much credit have you had experience paying back? If you have only had a revolving credit card with a $500 credit line a creditor would be hesitant to extend a $50,000 loan without the addition of a co-borrower or co-signer and significant income to prove ability to pay the debt.

What is your credit score? The above mentioned items are a few of the factors which help to determine your credit score. This can range from 300-850. Most credit scores fall between 600 and 750. This data is collected by three major reporting agencies. It is recommended that you review these regularly for accuracy and especially before any major purchases. Keep in mind this score can be reviewed when being considered for employment, advancement at work, obtaining an apartment, to access home utilities and much more.

Contact information for the 3 major Credit Bureaus

Equifax
Equifax.com/personal/credit-report-services
800-685-1111

Experian
Experian.com/help
888-397-3742

Transunion
TransUnion.com/credit-help
888-909-8872

Business Credit Agencies:

Duns & Bradstreet
https://www.dandb.com/contact-us/
800-700-2733

Equifax Small Business
www.equifax.com/business

Experian Business
https://sbcr.experian.com/

Nine Steps to Establishing Your Business Credit

1. **Incorporate your business.** With sole proprietorships and general partnerships, the business is legally the same as the owner; therefore, there can be no separation of business credit history from personal. Incorporating a business or forming an LLC creates a business that is legally separate from the owner(s).
2. **Obtain a federal tax employer identification number (EIN).** The EIN is basically a social security number for a business. It is required on federal tax filings, and is also required to open a business bank account in the name of the corporation or LLC. In order to comply with IRS requirements, many larger businesses also require an EIN from their vendors in order to pay them for services provided.
3. **Open a business bank account.** Open a business checking account in the legal business name. Once open, be sure to pay the financial transactions of the business from that account. Do not co-mingle personal expenses in business account. That puts you at risk if ever sued. If you use a business credit card (see below) for many financial transactions, be sure to pay the credit card bill from your business checking account.
4. **Establish a business phone number.** Whether you use a landline, cell phone or VoIP, have a separate number for your business in your business' legal name. List that number in the directory so it can be found.
5. **Open a business credit file.** Open a business credit file with the two business reporting agencies: Experian and Equifax.
6. **Establish a DUNS Account-** This is necessary when pursuing government contract.

7. **Obtain business credit card(s).** Obtain at least one business credit card that is not linked to you or any other owners personally. Pick a business credit card from a company that reports to the credit reporting agencies.
8. **Establish a line of credit with vendors or suppliers.** Work with vendors and/or suppliers to create credit for your company to use when purchasing with them. Ask them to report your payment history to the credit reporting agencies.
9. **Pay your bills on time.** This should be obvious but I am going to say it anyway. Be sure to pay your bills on time. Like with your personal credit, late payments will negatively impact your business credit.

Simple Steps to Restoring Credit

1. PAY ALL BILLS ON TIME!

2. Try to pay twice a month-this lowers the interest you are charged in the month. Just break the payment up into two payments. (Exp. $100 payment= pay $50 on 1st and $50 on 15th)

3. If you can pay 3 times the monthly payment this can boost your credit score quickly. (Exp. $25 payment= pay $75 in one month) This causes your score to jump around 20 to 30 points over 2 months. The more you do this the faster it goes up.

4. If a credit card bill is older than 6 months old leave it alone unless you are ready to pay it off. The damage it has caused has already happened. However, if it is a phone bill or utility please pay as soon as possible because they will keep selling the debt until you do. You can usually offer a settlement on these.

5. Don't be afraid to settle an old debt when you can. For instance if you owe $600 and have $300, inform the creditor that you can pay $300. If it has been some time they will usually accept it. Just make sure you get the agreement in writing and keep record of it.

6. If it is a new collection reach out to the creditor immediately to see what programs they have to

help. They may be able to lower interest and waive past due. Just communicate.

Leverage the Expertise of Others

The fastest way to get burnt out in a business is to try to do everything yourself. A successful business owner focuses on what they do best and hire others to do the rest. This allows the business owner the time necessary to invest in their craft without distractions and the pressure of trying to be an expert in another area. It reduces error and inefficiency due to trying to navigate the unfamiliar. For example, a chef would not seat guests and manage their wait staff while trying to prepare the meals. They would concentrate on their expertise.

Here are a few experts that should be a part of your team. They do not have to be a part of your regular payroll but should be accessible when needed.

Mentor- An advisor in the field of industry to guide and help new entrepreneurs make connections and avoid unnecessary missteps in their business. A great resource to find one would be through www.score.org. Free service

Bookkeeper- Ensures that all of a company's expenses, income and transactions are recorded and reconcile the company's financial accounts on a monthly or quarterly basis. Bookkeepers might also help with financial statement and financial report preparation.

Business Attorney- Concentrates their practice on problems that affect companies, such as intellectual property, different types of business transactions, and taxation. They may write up legal documents, negotiate the terms of a settlement, or argue their clients' cases in court as well as prepares and review contracts for businesses.

Business Banker- Oversees the transactions in the business account. You need to develop a relationship with your banker as they can advise of new accounts you may be eligible for as well as notify you of resources to help your business grow.

CPA- Certified Public accountant provides a range of accounting services, auditing, tax, and consulting tasks for corporations, small businesses, non-profit organizations, governments, and individuals. Any qualified public accountant can do most of these tasks; however, a CPA can do two things that an accountant without a CPA license cannot:

1. Prepare audited or reviewed financial statements and file a report with the Securities and Exchange Commission (SEC). All public companies must file audited financial statements with the SEC.
2. Represent clients in front of the Internal Revenue Service. (However, a non-CPA who is an attorney, enrolled agent, enrolled retirement plan agent, or enrolled actuary can also represent clients.)

What are Creditors Reviewing?

After developing the business plan and evaluating all the cost you may find that you need to obtain financing. What are the creditors reviewing? Below is a chart that helps us to simplify this process.

Character/Credit	Capacity	Capital
Are you honest and reliable? Creditor will look at your past experience with credit to see if you have late or irregular payment habits. The more diverse types and length of time the better. Were you difficult to reach in the application phase?	Are you able to meet your personal and business monthly expenses and all other debt payments (credit card, other loans, mortgage) using your existing sources of income?	What have you invested into your business? Capital represents savings, your time, money, and business assets.

Collateral	Conditions	Character/Credit
Business assets owned or to be purchased that will be used to secure the loan.	What is the current climate in the economy? Is the market saturated in that industry?	Measures reliability
		Capacity
		Measures your ability to repay
		Capital
		Measures your commitment
		Collateral
		Measures what you own
	Experience	Conditions
	What is your relevant experience within the industry?	Measures market reception
		Experience
		Measures past history

Pitfalls to Avoid

As you become more successful you will notice that some people will gravitate towards you and others will avoid you. You need to remain focused and allow those who do not share your vision or encourage your growth to move on. Holding on to relationships that limit you will also limit your success. Instead, surround yourself with positive and supportive individuals who will help you achieve your goals and encourage you to keep going despite the challenges.

Do not allow your vision to blind you! What this means is that when your business is not profitable and has not made a profit after a year of personally funding it, you may want to reconsider that the timing may be off, product may not be as widely accepted as you think, or your target market may not be correct. In these instances, some reevaluation must take place. Either you need to bring on a non-biased individual to look at the overall business and see if you are on track to grow or if it is time to pull out so you don't eventually bleed your personal income dry. Remember, many of our most successful business owners had failed attempts before achieving success. They did not give up but had to alter their vision.

Waiting too long to seek funding can be a pitfall. Some business owners fear getting into debt which sometimes limit the growth potential of the business. They may inherit or obtain a large sum of money and decide that they want to open a business but later find out that they do not have enough to complete the project and finally seek funding. This is not the time to seek funding. The best time to obtain funding is when you have money in the bank and have a continuous income flow coming in. Essentially, don't quit your day job before seeking funding and don't exhaust your savings. Creditors see these things as your lifeline should you meet some unexpected challenges which often happens when starting a business.

A Successful Outcome

A successful business owner must understand that they may be a sole owner business but they should never be in business by themselves. What does this mean? Simply, that you need others to help you promote your business. If no one knows you exist you will not be successful. Take advantage of all avenues to build a network of supporters for your business. The more people that know about your business the better the chances are for your business to succeed.

Here are some strategies to help you achieve a successful outcome in your business.

Join a chamber and be active in that chamber. If you are just listed in their directory and do not attend any events or participate in some of their activities you have wasted money. A listing by itself will not draw people to your business.

Utilize Social Media. Notice I stated utilize it. Do not just have one that is inactive. You want to promote traffic to your social media leading to your business. Feature a new product each week. Have a sale. Do something to drive interest on a weekly basis to your business.

Market your business. You need to invest in advertising your business in some form. If you are not going to spend the money on marketing you will spend it with your time physically marketing by word of mouth. Either way it will cost you. You just have to decide if you want to use your time or your money. My preference is both but as your business grows you should redirect your time to the operation of the business and put dollars into your marketing.

Partner with related businesses. This strategy helps each of you to promote both of your businesses to your clients. For instance if you are a winery you can partner with a restaurant that will serve your wine. You can then market their restaurant for the perfect pairing.

Network- Get out of your business and make sure that you are attending local business groups. Look for opportunity in the community to talk about your business and meet other business owners.

Remember people do business with people they like and know. Make yourself known by trying some of these strategies.

Useful Business Resources

Copyright Information
www.copyright.gov

Market Research
https://cbb.census.gov/sbe

The Occupational Health and Safety Administration
www.osha.gov

Patent Registration and Information
www.uspto.gov/inventors

Request Employer Identification Number
https://www.irs.gov/businesses/small-businesses-self-employed/employer-id-numbers

SCORE Mentors
https://www.score.org/find-mentor

Small Business Association
www.sba.gov

Small Business Development Center
https://www.sba.gov/offices/headquarters/osbdc

Glossary

Bylaws-a rule adopted by an organization chiefly for the government of its members and the regulation of its affairs.

Co-borrower- an additional borrower whose name appears on loan documents who shares equal financial and credit obligations to the loan. They are usually required if income is not sufficient. They usually have a share of ownership in business or shares the same household expenses as main borrower.

Co-Signer- An individual who personally guarantees a loan. This is usually required to mitigate credit risk. This individual does not need to have a percentage of ownership.

Crowdfunding- The use of small amounts of capital from a large number of individuals to finance a new business venture.

Limited Liability Company, (LLC) - a business structure in the United States whereby the owners are not personally liable for the company's debts or liabilities.

Operating Agreement- a document that customizes the terms of a limited liability company according to the specific needs of its owners. It also outlines the financial and functional decision-making in a structured manner.

Revolving Credit- credit that is automatically renewed as debts are paid off.

SCORE- A network of expert business volunteers who provide mentoring and guidance to start-up and small business owners.

Term Loan- a thing that is borrowed, especially a sum of money that is expected to be paid back with interest.

Trade Line- a record of activity for any type of credit extended to a borrower and reported to a credit reporting agency.

Acknowledgement

I would like to thank Dr. Sinclair N. Grey III, author, speaker and success coach for mentoring me through this process of writing my first book. A great testimony of why we need mentors to avoid unnecessary pitfalls.

Notes:

_____

_____

_____

_____

_____

_____

_____

_____

_____

_____

_____

_____

_____

Notes:

Notes:

Notes:

_____

_____

_____

_____

_____

_____

_____

_____

_____

_____

_____

_____

_____

www.ingramcontent.com/pod-product-compliance
Lightning Source LLC
Chambersburg PA
CBHW030549220526
45463CB00007B/3040